WRITE A BOOK
IN A YEAR
Writing Workshop & Workbook

Jacinta McDevitt

fuchsia

Published 2006
By Fuchsia Publishing
fuchsiapublishing@hotmail.com
01 8452298

The moral right of the author has been asserted.

Typesetting, layout, design © Fuchsia Publishing.

ISBN-10: 0-9553858-0-6
ISBN-13: 978-0-9553858-0-3

Designed by create: *www.create.ie*
Printed by Inkspot

www.jacintamcdevitt.com

About the Author

I live in Malahide, County Dublin. I have two grown up children and three novels under my belt "SIGNS ON", "HANDLE WITH CARE" and "EXCESS BAGGAGE". My novels were published by Poolbeg.

Next year is going to be a hectic one for me as I am being given two new titles.

My son, Alan and his wife, Máire are going to be responsible for giving me the title Granny in the new year and my daughter, Lucy is giving me the title Mother-of-the-Bride when she marries Conor in August 2007.

Days to treasure, always.

For Alan & Lucy – endless love, this is the one I promised you.
Also for Máire, Conor, Mam & Dad, and Brian with all my
love, always.

Jacinta

"I, not events, have the power to make me happy or unhappy today.
I can choose what it shall be.
Yesterday is dead,
Tomorrow hasn't arrived yet.
I have but one day, and I am going to be happy in it."

Groucho Marx

I'm Jacinta...

Welcome to my writing workshop.

"*Words are, of course, the most powerful drug used by mankind.*"

Rudyard Kipling

I have been involved in giving many, many writing workshops. When I started giving workshops I was amazed and surprised at the wonderful writing each workshop produced. Now I still marvel at the wonderful writing but I am no longer surprised by it. It is a pleasure and a privilege for me to be there when people discover that they can write. I am honoured when they share their stories with me.

I receive lots of enquiries from people wanting to attend workshops but through circumstance of distance or other commitments cannot attend. So, I am now bringing my workshop to you. The good news is you don't have to leave the comfort of your home to join this workshop.

The wonderful thing about books is that they are portable, I have made my workshop portable by putting it in book form. You can now do my workshop wherever you want and whenever you want. You can bring it on holiday with you or even do it in your pyjamas curled up in bed. You can do it when the house is untidy, you can even do it when a pile of ironing is beckoning or grass needs mowing. The important thing is to put off the ironing and the mowing rather than the writing. Write wherever it suits you. You decide. You can do this workshop all in one sitting or bit-by-bit. Whatever way you do it is the right way to do it.

The bad news is:

YOU NO LONGER HAVE AN EXCUSE NOT TO WRITE.

In doing this workshop you will see that:

YOU ARE A STORYTELLER.	YOU CAN CREATE SETTINGS.
YOU ARE CREATIVE.	YOU CAN CREATE PLOT.
YOU CAN WRITE.	YOU CAN WRITE A BOOK.
YOU CAN CREATE CHARACTERS.	

So, if you are one of those people who:

☛ *Have the longing to write but keep putting it on the long finger;*
☛ *Keep saying, "I'll start tomorrow";*
☛ *Want to write a novel you've been thinking about for ages;*
☛ *Have a story to tell but don't have the confidence to tell it;*
☛ *Just want to try something different and new.*

Then without a doubt:

THIS IS THE WRITING WORKSHOP FOR YOU.
THIS WRITING WORKSHOP WORKS.

This writing workshop *&* workbook is not just any book on writing. Neither is it the definitive book on writing or on the rules of writing. It's not even an analysis of writing. It is an action workbook. A workbook to get you to write and to help you step by step along the way. My workshop *&* workbook is what I believe you need to know and do to get writing and to keep going. Over the course of this workshop I will give you the tools you need to write, the encouragement to write and the confidence and enthusiasm to keep going. So, whether you are a complete novice to writing or have been doing it for a while, whether you keep all your characters to yourself or share them with a writers group, this workshop *&* workbook will help you. If you are interested in writing this is the book for you. If you want to try something new, try this workbook.

Firstly, I will tell you about me and how I write and then I will lead you gently into another world with new people to meet and places to see. A world you will create yourself. The bad news is that I don't have a magic wand to give you and, Abracadabra!, you have a book written in a year. But I promise I do have something much better than any magic wand. I have a magic formula. And today because you are taking that first brave step and starting my workshop, because I'm in such a great mood and because it's such a wonderful day and just because I'm such a nice person, I will share my magic formula with you.

Yes, I promise I will reveal my magic formula. If you use the magic formula you will have a book written in one year. Yes, that's right – a year. Simply follow my magic formula. However, if I give you my magic formula you have to promise me that you will use it. I cannot cope with the thoughts of my poor little magic formula just lying in a drawer gathering dust or shoved into the back of some book or hidden away somewhere unused. You must promise to use it. I'm going to hold you to that promise – I promise.

Once you have finished this workshop *&* workbook, each and every one of you will know that you can write. You will know that you can write that book you've been threatening to write for a long, long time or the one you've only just thought about today. You will have my secret magic formula that will guarantee you write that book in one year.

Well done you for taking the first step.

Now, turn over the page and come along with me step by step.

What I did

*"A journey
of a thousand
miles begins with
a single step."*

Confucius

So, to begin with the easy part, where I do the talking and tell you a little bit about myself and how I ended up writing.

I am first and foremost a reader. I love books. I love the feel and the smell of the paper and the look of all the words on the page. I love wondering who has read a book before me if it's a borrowed book, or taking pleasure in being the first to open the pages of a brand new book.

In this day of plug-in everything and hi-tech every other thing, it's great for a person like me, who has an allergy to machines, (except dishwashers which get my number one vote), to be able to open a book and be transported to somewhere else, share someone else's problems for a while or laugh and cry with all the new characters I'll meet along the way. Books are portable, great entertainment, sheer escapism and free if you happen to be a member of the library.

Kelly the main character in my second book, "HANDLE WITH CARE," says of books:

> *"I loved the sheer escapism of it all. The participation and enjoyment I got from anyone else's life but my own. I loved to go into a world of fiction where everyone had problems. I took comfort from the fact that their problems were sometimes worse than mine and yet they were always solved by the end of the book and all the characters always lived happily ever after. I reasoned that if some people with horrendous lives got everything sorted in the space of a few chapters then surely be to God I would."*

My own first memory of books is as a very, very young child, tucked up in bed listening to my parents reading us bedtime stories. The tales enraptured me.

When I was a young girl I did my first bit of writing. I wrote a comic for my younger brother and sister. I called it Cindy which is my nickname. It had picture stories and competitions and even fashion tips!

When I had children of my own I brought them to the library, bought them books and told them bedtime stories, out of my head, or my brain, as my children used to say. While I was very grateful to them for noticing that their mother did indeed have a brain, the trouble was that if they asked me for the same story twice, they remembered details that I had forgotten. So I started writing them down.

I was a speech and drama teacher and I started writing sketches for my students to perform. But I never looked upon any of this as "proper" writing, I know now that of course, it was. At that time too I started going to talks etc. that were given by writers – purely from a reader's point of view. Then I did a writing course and found I loved it. My interest in writing had come directly from my love of reading.

I started writing short stories and sent one to Woman's Way, "NO PLACE LIKE IT". They published it. I sent another, "TOE BROKE OR NOT TOE BROKE", which they published also. The then editor, Celine Naughton, rang and asked me to send them in another. I wrote "SHOP TILL YOU DROP". Then they asked me to write a series of articles called "THAT'S LIFE". These articles were a quirky look at life. I loved doing this.

At the same time I was entering lots of competitions and was thrilled when I was short-listed or placed. Having a story broadcast on RTÉ for the Francis McManus Awards was terrific (WAY TO GO, DAD). All of this gave me great encouragement to keep writing. *(I have included some of these stories at the back of this workbook.)*

Just as I was getting published and doing well in competitions and starting on the writing road I fell down the stairs and broke my leg. Now I'm not suggesting you all try this, but it worked very well for me! It was my lucky break. I had to take time off work and was bored silly. I started writing my first book "SIGN'S ON". Poolbeg published it in July 2002. My second "HANDLE WITH CARE" was published in July 2003 and "EXCESS BAGGAGE" in 2004. I started giving talks and workshops and maybe because of my speech and drama teaching background I found I loved giving them. I have loved every minute of writing this workshop & workbook. It has been a true labour of love. I hope it helps you or at the very least gives you the hope and confidence to weather the storm and let your story loose into the world.

So, now it's your turn. Today is the day you start making the same journey I did. **Today is the day you start writing.**

Writing is communicating, relating information and telling stories. We are all storytellers. Since time began we have told stories. It all started with Adam and Eve and their antics in the garden – the first romantic story. Add in the sudden need for fig leaves and you have humourous romance. And a bit of a romantic thriller when the intrigue of the snake comes into the plot.

Everyday we relate things to one another. We ask each other "Any news?" We swap stories and exchange anecdotes everyday. We tell the story of our lives on a daily basis. Just think about yesterday and all the stories you exchanged with family, friends, work colleagues and even strangers in shops or queues. We are all storytellers at heart. The problem is getting it from your heart onto the paper.

The old well-used saying that writing is 99% perspiration and 1% inspiration is true. If you don't plant your backside on the chair to write you'll never start, never mind finish, anything. If you keep finding excuses not to start, you are not alone. Don't worry, most of us find some excuse not to start. There is always that pile of ironing, grass to be mowed, child to be bathed, baby to be fed or window to be stared out of. Life seems to get in the way.

We imagine that writing will take up too much time so we put it off until we have lots of time. But let's face it, we never have lots of time on our hands and if we do, we find something else to do with that time. Usually something for someone else. So, today I'm going to ask – no I'm going to insist, for your own good – that you take at least half an hour for yourself every day. I know that's doable. Let's face it, we all sit and watch programmes on TV that last a half an hour. A lunch break is usually an hour long. Half an hour isn't that hard to find. Take a half an hour at least for yourself and your writing everyday. It's all about choices.

If I could only give you only one piece of advice I would say to you – write something every day. Have a notebook with you wherever you go and write even a sentence every day. Writing makes you write. Writing makes you write. Writing makes you write. No it's not a misprint. It's so important it's worth repeating. Sit at your computer and write anything. Or get out a pen and notebook or, if you're really stuck, you can use an envelope or any scrap of paper. The important thing is that you write, even if it's only for five minutes every day. But try to give yourself half an hour.

The rest of the time, as you go about your daily routine, taking children to school, driving to work etc. etc. you can have "thinking time" where you mull the story around in your head. Where your character goes around with you and lives with you and you know every breath they take. Jot things down as you go along. Don't rely on your memory. You will forget those choice phrases, plot or characters that pop into your mind. Write them down.

I love notebooks and always have one with me. I have been lost on the one or two occasions when I forgot my notebook and have been known to write on chewing gum wrappers and menus. It's OK writing on these but reading it back later on is really hard work.

And you never know how you will be rewarded for having your notebook at the ready. In the queue to board a flight recently at Dublin Airport there was none other than our own Colin Farrell in the queue ahead of me waiting to board the plane. I searched my bag and found my latest notebook – in the shape of a black satin corset with red fur trim. I sidled up to Colin and quietly asked him if he'd be the first man to sign my corset. He said he'd be delighted and why wouldn't he be. He was lovely and were it not for the notebook I might never have asked him – sure you couldn't ask our Colin to sign any ol' scrap of paper now could you? As an aside I have to say that he is stunningly good looking in the flesh so to speak. Anyway, he's terrific looking and was really nice to all us more mature ladies that were swooning over him. I will never listen to a bad word said against our Colin. Who knows you could be about to write a novel that will be turned into a screenplay starring our own Colin.

Now there's another reason for you to get cracking.

STEP
THREE

*My Magic
Formula*

*"It is not a bad
idea to get in the
habit of writing
down one's
thoughts. It
saves one having
to bother anyone
else with them."*

Isabel Colegate

I am asked many questions about writing at workshops, talks and by email. I am delighted to answer them all. One question that comes up again and again is about wordage in a novel.

"How many words do I have to write to write a novel?" They ask.

"About 150,000 words." I say.

"Are you mad? That's a huge amount! How in the name of God could anyone write that much?" they say back, in shock and horror.

So today, as a special treat and because I promised you, I'm going to let you all in on my little secret. I am also going to give you My Magic Formula. Remember, if I give you the Magic Formula you have to use it. I promise it will make you write that book in a year, it will also help you every time you get stuck and it will keep your goal in sight. It has magical powers that you can't begin to imagine.

My secret is...

Wait for it...

It actually only takes 410 words to write a novel.
That's right, only 410.
Not a lot. Is it?
"I can do that." I hear you all thinking.
And you can, anyone can do it.
Just 410 words.

I promise you... if you write 410 words you will end up with a novel. *"What's the catch?"* Again I can hear you thinking, that's the thing about this workbook *&* workshop I can hear you thinking all the way through it.

So let me tell you there is no catch there is only:

My Magic Formula

410 (WORDS) X 365 (DAYS) = 1 (BOOK)

I promise that if you write only 410 words every day at the end of a year you will have 149,650 words. Put these words between two covers and you will have a book in a year.

So, now you're thinking: "So, if I write 820 words a day I'd have a book written in six months?" Well, that's right too but let's not get ahead of ourselves. We want 410 **great** words not 820 **rushed** ones. Let's not walk before we can crawl and let's walk before we run. Let's do what's doable first and if you find you're doing more well, then, that's a bonus. Remember, it's not a race.

And guess what? Yes, you guessed it – this whole piece on My Magic Formula is exactly 410 words. I know you're going to count each and every one of them!

The Contract

I will give you all the encouragement and the tools to write but before the writing begins I want you to make the commitment. Make a contract with yourself. Make yourself a promise and keep it.

I

(your name)

DO SOLEMNLY PROMISE
THAT FROM TODAY:

__/__/__

(date)

I WILL:

A) WRITE 410 WORDS EVERYDAY.

B) CARRY A NOTEBOOK &
PEN WITH ME EVERYWHERE.

C) COMPLETE THIS
WORKBOOK & WORKSHOP.

Now armed with my secret formula and your contract you're ready – let the writing begin.

Step Five

Setting Goals

> *"Nothing can stop the man with the right mental attitude from achieving his goal; nothing on earth can help the man with the wrong mental attitude."*

Thomas Jefferson

Now you are armed with the magic formula it will stand you in good stead throughout your writing and cure many ills.

The magic formula will help you achieve all your goals.

The first goal is to **start**
The second goal is to **keep going**
The third goal is to **finish**

These are achievable goals. Goals to be proud of and relish in. 410 words per day will enable you to achieve all three goals.

410 words per day will end the frustration if you get stuck, getting stuck will no longer be something to worry about. Whenever you feel you have writer's block, just get out a piece of paper or sit at your computer and instead of writing nothing, write 410 words on anything you like. Write about whatever is on the table beside you, what you can see out the window or even how you are feeling. Write down all your frustrations and delights. Just write what comes into your head. By the time you have finished writing 410 words you will see that you no longer have writer's block. If you manage to prove me wrong and still have a block then write 410 more words. This will free up your ideas and free up your writing.

Over the page there is a list of goals. Cross off each one as you achieve it. You should cross one off every day.

start	410	410	410	410	410	410	410	410	410	410	410
410	410	410	410	410	410	410	410	410	410	410	410
410	410	410	410	410	410	410	410	410	410	410	410
410	410	410	410	410	410	410	410	410	410	410	410
410	410	410	410	410	410	410	410	410	410	410	410
410	410	410	410	410	410	410	410	410	410	410	410
410	410	410	410	410	410	410	410	410	410	410	410
410	410	410	410	410	410	410	410	410	410	410	410
410	410	410	410	410	410	410	410	410	410	410	410
410	410	410	410	410	410	410	410	410	410	410	410
410	410	410	410	410	410	410	410	410	410	410	410
410	410	410	410	410	410	410	410	410	410	410	410
410	410	410	410	410	410	410	410	410	410	410	410
410	410	410	410	410	410	410	410	410	410	410	410
410	410	410	410	410	410	410	410	410	410	410	410
410	410	410	410	410	410	410	410	410	410	410	410

410	410	410	410	410	410	410	410	410	410	410	410
410	410	410	410	410	410	410	410	410	410	410	410
410	410	410	410	410	410	410	410	410	410	410	410
410	410	410	410	410	410	410	410	410	410	410	410
410	410	410	410	410	410	410	410	410	410	410	410
410	410	410	410	410	410	410	410	410	410	410	410
410	410	410	410	410	410	410	410	410	410	410	410
410	410	410	410	410	410	410	410	410	410	410	410
410	410	410	410	410	410	410	410	410	410	410	410
410	410	410	410	410	410	410	410	410	410	410	410
410	410	410	410	410	410	410	410	410	410	410	410
410	410	410	410	410	410	410	410	410	410	410	410
410	410	410	410	410	410	410	410	410	410	410	410
410	410	410	410	410	410	410	410	410	410	410	410
410	410	410	410	410	410	*finish*					

As in life itself the best thing in your writing is to be honest. Be honest to yourself and your reader. Don't try to copy someone else's writing. You are unique, be your unique self. You have something different to offer and that's your own uniqueness and difference. That uniqueness and difference is the very thing that will make you stand out. It's no good to ape someone else – you won't be able to sustain it and the reader won't be fooled by it. Your own voice will flow and come naturally for you.

You owe it to the reader who has taken the time and parted with their hard-earned cash to be as honest as you can in your writing.

Your voice is as unique as you are. It's your stamp on the page. It's your innards pouring into the story and it's all yours. No one else can feel or write the way you can. Rejoice in it.

Find your voice and the words will flow.

So how do you find your voice?

Simple – write, write and write some more. Let the real you do the writing forget about writing for an audience or to sell books or impress a publisher. Just keep it honest and true and that will follow.

Don't worry, your own voice is not buried too deep, you use it all the time in everyday life. It's part of you and it loves to come to the surface. It wants to be heard.

Now I want you to write. I want you to tell me all about your favourite things. What's your favourite thing to do in your spare time? your favourite holidays? foods and drink? favourite book and film? Favourite people. Tell me everything. All your favourites. Just keep going.

Write down whatever comes into your head as it comes into your head. Keep going. Let it flow. Let it all pour out of you. Keep going until you have finished. Don't worry about punctuation. This is free writing and it is a great tool.

"Even in literature and art, no man who bothers about originality will ever be original: Whereas if you simply try to tell the truth (without caring twopence how often it has been told before) you will, nine times out of ten, become original without ever having noticed it."

C. S. Lewis

Well done you've just done your first bit of writing.
If you followed the instructions you have also found your voice.

*"I saw the angel
in the marble
and carved until
I set him free."*

*Michaelangelo
Buonarroti*

Character

No I'm not referring to a pop group when I say the who. I'm referring to people, characters. I firmly believe that characters are one of the most important, if not the most important element in fiction. You must get your reader to believe in your characters and to do that, you must believe in them.

Your reader doesn't have to know every tiny detail about your character but you should. If you can see your character as a real person your reader will too. When you get to know your characters well enough they will tell you where the story is going. Live with them. Go around with them constantly in your head. Let them haunt you.

If any of the characters in my books were to walk in here now, I would instantly know them. I lived with them long enough. Sometimes after I have finished a book, I miss them dreadfully. In the book I am writing at the moment I have become so attached to my character that I'm going to have to force myself to let her go. She's a class act.

My characters are never based on anyone. I created them. I know exactly what they will do or say in any given situation. I know too what they are not capable of.

So where do these characters come from? They can be found anywhere but mostly they come from:

1. INSIDE YOURSELF

2. OUTSIDE INFLUENCES

3. MIRACULOUSLY

1. **Inside yourself** – characters can come from something within ourselves, some gesture, some turn of phrase, some physical or personality trait that triggers our imagination and a character is born.

2. **Outside influence** – characters can also come from some trait or nuance or foible of someone we see.

3. And most delicious of all are the characters who arrive **miraculously**, whole and entire all by themselves and unannounced. This is wonderful and happens more often than you'd think.

In writing fiction never be tempted to write about a real person that you know. It can be very limiting and the person you choose may recognise themselves. I broke this rule once on purpose. I wrote a story called "LOVE ME TENDER" *(see final chapter)* and I used my children's names and their personality traits. I wanted to write something about them. The story is pure fiction but the personalities are my children's. When I finished writing the story, I let them read it and they liked it. I guess they were delighted I didn't write about them in their teenage years!!

No matter what way your characters arrive you need to nurture them and let them grow into fully rounded people that will tell their story. The best way to do this is to make a character profile with every little detail you can. In building your profile in your own notes you cannot be too detailed – moles, birthmarks etc. You might never mention them in your book but you should know them.

As well as physical appearance, you must know the characters' nuances and if they have any little foibles. Any characteristic which makes them unique.

Are they witty, sexy, bitchy, boring etc. etc?

Mannerisms usually don't change throughout a person's lifetime the way their bodies do. Hence the saying "you haven't changed a bit" even though you are 30 years older.

One more thing – it is a rarity to find a person who is 100% good. It's better to reflect this. Give them some human frailty albeit a nice one with which your reader can identify. Any book I have read that has a character who is a chocoholic and always trying to diet is very easy for me to identify with!!

Someone else may identify with a skinny person trying to gain a few pounds. Lucky them I say. Try to identify with your character. If you can, your reader will.

Remember it is also a rarity for a person to be 100% bad. Most people have some saving grace – reflect this. In the same way, remember to give your bad characters a little bit of humanity. Not too much or you'll confuse the reader. Once the reader believes in the character, then anything is possible. By the time the reader gets to the end of the story they should feel they have met someone new.

Create a Character

On the next page you will see two lists with all the information you need to create your character. Just fill in the lists. Put only one or two words beside each trigger word, no more. In some cases I have given you choices. Later on you will use these lists to make your character.

Here's an example:

CHARACTER NAME: **Rebecca**

Physical Traits

Sex: female

Age: 30*ish*

Height: 5.7

Weight: 10 stone

Build: skinny

Hair: *(type/colour/length)* black with a bit of a curl/shoulder length

Eyes: *(colour/glasses)* blue eyes/glasses/sometimes contact lenses

Facial hair: *(moustache/beard)* n/a

Eyebrows: *(bushy/plucked/pencilled)* finely plucked

Skin colour: natural tanned

Nationality: Irish

Now I want you to fill in your own character lists.

CHARACTER NAME: _____

Physical Traits

Sex:
Age:
Height: *(tall/small/average)*
Weight: *(thin/average/curvy/overweight/obese)*
Build:
Hair: *(type/colour/length)*
Eyes: *(colour/glasses)*
Facial hair: *(moustache/beard)*
Eyebrows: *(bushy/plucked/pencilled)*
Mouth: *(thin lipped/etc.)*
Dimples:
Moles:
Scars:
Skin colour:
Nationality:
Other:

Personality and stage of life

Marital Status:
Family:
Where they live: *(house/apartment etc.)*
Profession:
Job:
Background:
Family circumstances:
Hobbies:
Interests:
Special needs:
Special skills:
Happy:
Grumpy:
Sad:
Short fuse:
Extrovert:
Introvert:
Shy:
Flamboyant:
Dramatic:
Other:

You can add to these lists as time goes on and you discover more about your character.

The Person, The Whole Person And Nothing But The Person

Now using the character's physical and personality profile I want you to write a short passage that describes your character to me.

You have given your character a name. Now describe them. There is no need to set a scene. Just tell me all about your character. Take from your lists. Let the character simmer in your head. Get to know them for a few minutes. Now create them, breathe life into them and make them real – tell me all about them. Spare no detail. No detail is too small. Don't force them. Let them do the work for you. Once you start writing, with all the knowledge you have of the character and in your own voice you will find it comes naturally.

My character's name is...

_____
_____
_____
_____
_____
_____
_____
_____
_____
_____
_____
_____
_____
_____
_____
_____
_____
_____
_____
_____
_____
_____
_____
_____
_____
_____
_____
_____
_____
_____
_____
_____
_____
_____
_____
_____
_____
_____
_____
_____
_____
_____
_____
_____
_____
_____
_____

Well done you have just created a character... Isn't this a lot easier than
you thought it would be? I want you to let the character live in your
head. Live with them. Get to know them. Enjoy them.
Now let's make them speak.

STEP
EIGHT

The Who **Talks**

*"I love talking
about nothing.
It's the only
thing I know
anything about."*

Oscar Wilde

Dialogue

Dialogue is the words you put into people's mouths. You must make their words be true to their character. You must make the language be true to the time setting you have chosen and indeed the place setting. For example, a fourteen year old boy from the inner city of Dublin in 2006 will use different language and turns-of-phrase to a 75 year old woman from an isolated village in the west of Ireland living a hundred years ago. Indeed the teenager of today would speak a lot differently to the teenager of 50 years ago.

Dialogue is very important. It moves the story and indirectly tells us so much about the characters, the situations. It is the conversation between the characters that give us an insight into them and what is happening, or as things happen or unfold, or even warn us of things that might be about to happen.

Avoid stilted conversation. The best way to do this is to read it aloud to yourself. This is great, particularly when you start writing. It tunes your inner ear and soon you will be able to hear the dialogue as you write it.

Be as natural as you can.

Dialogue also gives us an insight into relationships and characters. The way we talk to each other in real life determines the relationship we have with people. We talk more casually to friends and family than to strangers or our boss etc. We tend to speak differently to children – we most certainly have different content in our speech with them.

Language has changed over the years. For example people today use more "bad" language than they would have in Victorian times. Yes, you must make sure that the language your characters use is appropriate for the time you have set them in but don't use bad language just for the sake of it. Let the dialogue be natural and you'll get the balance right.

We use different language to give instructions or directions than we use for invitations or praise. Our language changes when reprimanding someone or indeed when we are sharing loving thoughts with someone. And depending on the level of reprimand or love our language changes yet again.

Language and dialogue should flow easily and be believable. Don't try to impress your reader with language or big words. Use the words and language your character would use. The words should express their emotion or tell us something. We reveal our thoughts and feelings through our use of language and words.

Don't have too many he said/she said. Once you have established who speaks first the reader knows the other person is answering.

TRY TO LET LANGUAGE PORTRAY EMOTION – SHOW US, DON'T TELL US.

Consider these:

"I'll make you a cup of tea." He said lovingly.
"I'll make you a nice cup of tea, darling."

The second one is much better and gives us an incite into the characters and their relationship. There is no need to keep saying, "he asked" just put in a question mark, ie. ? No need to keep saying, "he exclaimed" just put in an exclamation mark, ie. !

Now it's your turn again. This time I want you to write a bit of dialogue just to get the feel of your character. You can have him/her at work or at home or in the shop or anywhere that he/she would be talking to another person.

For any of you that need an idea, how about getting her/him to be in a restaurant. They can be with a group of friends or work colleagues or one friend in particular of the same or opposite sex. You can pick something from My Favourites piece that you did earlier on in the workshop and have a conversation about all the things or some of them.

In Conversation With...

"A place for
everything, and
everything in
its place."

Benjamin
Franklin

Setting

Now you have a feel for your character, I cannot say it often enough how important it is to let your characters haunt you. Let them be with you all the time. You have created them and given them a voice. The wonderful thing about writing is that you can have as many imaginary friends as you like and no one will think you are crazy.

Now let's place your main character. Let's look at the when and the where or the setting as it's called.

WHAT TIME IS THE CHARACTER LIVING IN? DON'T TELL US SHOW US.

In the opening of my first book "SIGN'S ON", Linda is at home. The washing machine is leaking. Her husband is watching telly. She has a bit of gossip and is dying to ring her best friend to tell her.

The when is modern times and the where is her home. The machinery tells us it's set in modern times and through language, dialogue and reference we know it's her home although we are never told the when and the where directly.

In "HANDLE WITH CARE", Kelly is on the steps of the divorce courts. The river Liffey and several buildings around Dublin are mentioned. It's Valentine's Day. Her best friend Phil rings her on the mobile phone.

Again the when is modern times. Divorce in Ireland and the mobile phone places us in that time frame. The where is Dublin, Ireland again because of language and reference.

In "EXCESS BAGGAGE", Emma is on a plane and again it's obvious from the start that it is set in modern times. The where is on a plane. Later the where changes to a small Italian island called Aronna (fictional) and to Dublin, Ireland. As a matter of fact, I received emails from people wanting to holiday there. Unfortunately, the island only existed in my head and in my book.

You can place your character in a setting without telling us directly. Once the setting is firmly in your own head and you visualise your character living and being in that setting, it will transfer onto the page. In everything they do and everything they say, the era of the novel will seep through.

From the character profile you have already done, you are aware of the background of your character and where they live, so you have already chosen a setting.

You don't have to mention your setting in the opening lines but by the end of the first chapter the reader needs to know the where and the when of the book.

So, drawing from the character profile you have already done and thinking about your character, I want you to tell me the where and the when of that character. I want you to be as exacting as you can. A lot of what you write now will not be in your novel but because you know it all, it will make your novel more believable. Write down the times your character is living in. Where they are living – describe it to me – the village or town, the house or apartment or caravan or wherever they live. Give me as much detail as you can. Write freely. Now if any of your book is going to be set in their place of work or abroad, describe that for me. Keep going.

The Where and When *(setting)*

*"The good ended
happily, and the
bad unhappily.
That is what
fiction means."*

Oscar Wilde

Plot

Now that you have the who, the where and the when sorted out, you need to consider the what and the why.

Some people start thinking of a novel with an idea for a character. For others, it's a plot. They get an idea of a plot and work characters into it. With me a character is always born first and then the plot. Whichever triggers your writing, all novels have characters and plot. The plot is a series of cause and effect events and how these affect the character and their loved ones.

I have found in all my workshops that people are fazed mostly with the word plot. They get bogged down in worrying about it. They worry about what there should be in a plot. Is the plot strong enough? Where should the plot go? Who or what drives the plot? And many more daunting thoughts. When some people hear "plot" they panic and get "block".

When I tell them that I prefer to use the word **story** instead of plot, there is instant relief. This might be sacrilegious to some writers, but for me it is less daunting. For me the plot of a novel is the story, the what and the why.

You are writing a story. Telling us all a story. As you progress with the story you will know where it's going. As each part unfolds it will take you deeper into the story. The way your characters deal with different situations becomes part of the story. They twist it and take it to places you never dreamed of when you first started.

You may wonder where you're going to get ideas from to write your story. Well you're surrounded by them. Everyone has a huge lucky bag of experience to draw from. If you feel you don't then just pick up a newspaper and see if there is some incident that triggers off a story for you.

Listen to all that is going on around you and you'll find yourself wondering what happened? Why did it happen?

Love is the thing most written about. Love of a man/woman. Mother/Father. Mother/father to Children. Sibling to Sibling. Friend to friend. Money. Land. Cars. Art. Golf. The list is endless. Romantic love is sometimes difficult for writers to write about. Where do we draw the line between writing about romance and love and writing about love making and sex. Well, it's easy really, just remember that no-one wants to read a biology lesson. If they did, they'd buy a science book. So avoid the biology lessons. Ryan Tubridy asked me on the radio recently how did I write "the dirty bits" – "I just sit back and enjoy it." I said. The best way to write them is as honestly as you can and make it fun. Avoid being too explicit.

We all want to be loved and to love. Your reader is no different. They will go along with your love scenes if you make them believable.

We are all intrigued with relationships and while we are indeed intrigued with our own personal relationships, we are more fascinated with the relationships of others. We like to be the fly on the wall. We like to read about others and how they handle things and what they do in given situations. These situations can arise from any thing or action or emotion. Emotions that affect the story can be greed, jealousy, revenge, duty, fear, vanity, envy, anger, loneliness, lust, pride, hate and so on and so on. Every human emotion can be used.

DON'T TELL US, SHOW US. YOU KNOW YOUR CHARACTER LEARN TO KNOW THEIR EMOTIONS.

"Write about what you know" is very good advice given to writers. However, this can be very restricting and shouldn't be taken literally. You don't have to limit yourself to only writing about what you have lived through in your own life. You can put yourself in someone else's shoes and use all your emotions to feel how that character would react and feel in a given situation. Many writers who write the most gruesome crime books haven't actually murdered anyone in their own lives and they are, in fact, the nicest people you could meet. They have great imaginations and do great research.

So what are the essential ingredients in a story?

Every story must have:

A BEGINNING = A SITUATION
A MIDDLE = A PROBLEM
AN END = A PROBLEM SOLVED

Let's hook the Beginning

The beginning of the story is where you set it all up. Where you tell us all we need to know in order for us to believe the problem you are going to give us later. In the beginning we get to meet the main character. The beginning is what makes the reader want to read on. We set the situation.

The hook is the thing that draws the reader in. The thing that makes them want to read the next chapter. The hook could be a character or a situation or a setting.

Let's meddle in the Middle

So now for the middle. The "What happens?" and "What happens next factor?"

We introduce a problem. Is someone killed, arrested, divorced, married, dead, born? Do they have an affair, are they sacked? All of the above. There are several ideas that are used, in various ways, time and time again in writing;

THE MONSTER – something/one is threatened. The town/world our own space or well being our family, friends, way of life, job. Our hero comes to save the day. Or we become our own hero and find a way to help ourselves.

RAGS TO RICHES – does what it says on the tin.

THE QUEST – we or someone we know or love needs something, a thing or emotional well being or love or happiness etc.

THE JOURNEY – either real or emotional.

TRAGEDY – where the eventual outcome is our hero's destruction maybe even by his own doing.

BORN AGAIN – where we start off as one thing and end up changed – physical or emotional.

GOOD V. EVIL – as obvious as it is, or disguised in some way

These are only a few of the topics and all are very general. They are good for ideas for starting a story.

I think the best thing to do is to begin your story and just keep asking yourself what happens next? What happens next? As the characters and the "what happens next?" factor grows in your head so too will the story.

So now we have:

THE BEGINNING – THE SITUATION – THE HOOK
THE MIDDLE - THE PROBLEM - WHAT HAPPENS NEXT?

We need the ending.

Let's enjoy the End
By the time the reader gets to the end of the book they shouldn't regret the time they spent reading the book or the money they spent buying the book.

It is always better to give some sort of hope to the reader at the end. We all love the feelgood factor. As a reader all I can say is, if you don't have an ending where all the loose ends are tied up and everyone is accounted for and not left miserable, you better have a very good reason for it.

So now we have:

A BEGINNING – A SITUATION - THE HOOK
A MIDDLE – A PROBLEM - THE WHAT HAPPENS NEXT?
THE END – PROBLEM SOLVED - THE AHH FACTOR

Now using the character you have created and the setting you have created I want you to write a summary of your story. You may change the story later but for the moment it will be your guide. Make sure you have a beginning, a middle and an end. A situation, a problem, a problem solved. Just write a small paragraph on each. Don't go on forever. Reserve your energy for later.

Beginning – a situation, a character, a setting.

_____
_____
_____
_____
_____
_____
_____
_____
_____
_____
_____
_____
_____
_____
_____
_____
_____
_____
_____
_____
_____
_____
_____
_____
_____
_____

Middle – a problem – what happens next? Keep asking.

_____
_____
_____
_____
_____
_____
_____
_____
_____
_____

End – solve the problem – the ahhh factor.

"*To accomplish
great things, we
must not only
act but also
dream. Not
only plan but
also believe.*"

Anatole France

You now have the who, the where and when and
the what and why of your novel. You also have a
main character. You have a summary of your story.
And you have the magic formula. You are all set.
Before you go full steam ahead I advise you to write
a plan.

In the same way as a dressmaker takes a pattern and
lays it on material and cuts out shapes that will
eventually be sewn together to form a garment you
now need a pattern to follow.

But not everyone is pattern size and the dressmaker
has to make nips and tucks along the way. You too
will have to make alterations along the way. You
too will have to tweak things every now and again.
But that's the great thing about a plan – you don't
have to stick to it.

I Love It When A Good Plan Comes Together

Let's make your novel have 36 chapters. Now fill in
the blanks. Put in a little bit about each chapter. If
you have some blanks that you can't fill in, that's
fine, you can go back and put it in later when you
know what you want to put into that chapter.

Chapter one
_____
_____
_____

Chapter two
_____
_____
_____

Chapter three
_____
_____
_____

Chapter four
_____
_____
_____

Chapter five

_____

_____

_____

Chapter six

_____

_____

Chapter seven

_____

_____

Chapter eight

_____

_____

Chapter nine

_____

_____

Chapter ten

_____

_____

Chapter eleven

_____

_____

Chapter twelve

_____

_____

Chapter thirteen

_____

_____

Chapter fourteen

_____

_____

Chapter fifteen

_____

_____

Chapter sixteen

Chapter seventeen

Chapter eighteen

Chapter nineteen

Chapter twenty

Chapter twenty-one

Chapter twenty-two

Chapter twenty-three

Chapter twenty-four

Chapter twenty-five

Chapter twenty-six

Chapter twenty-seven

Chapter twenty-eight

Chapter twenty-nine

Chapter thirty

Chapter thirty-one

Chapter thirty-two

Chapter thirty-three

Chapter thirty-four

Chapter thirty-five

Chapter thirty-six

*Now Just
Keep Going*

"*Finish each day
And be done
with it, You have
done what you
could, Some
blunders and
Absurdities have
crept in, Forget
them as soon
as you can
Tomorrow is a
new day, You
shall begin it
serenely, And
with too high a
spirit To be
encumbered
by Your old
nonsense.*"

*Ralph
Waldo
Emerson*

All writers, from the best-selling to the complete novices, from the writer starting the adventure of their first book to the writer starting the adventure of their tenth, begin the same way. We all begin with a blank page, an empty screen. We all have to start a book by putting the first word on the page and then the second and the third and so on. We are all the same and you are no different. All of us start by words, sentences, paragraphs, chapters, a beginning, a middle and an end. A novel. The difference between starting a book and finishing a book is simple – just keep going.

From doing this workbook & workshop you now have:

A CHARACTER
A SETTING
A STORY
A PLAN

*And most importantly of all you now have:
A Magic Formula*

Now I want you to go back to your chapter plan – read what you have written for chapter one – sit at the PC or take up your notebook and write:

A STORY BY:

(your name) _____

Chapter 1

Now you no longer have a blank page.

Looking at what you have written for Chapter 1 in your plan begin to write your first 410 words.

Congratulations

You have just started your book – follow my steps and my magic formula and before you know where you are you'll be finished. Remember to use your goal chart and cross off each 410 box.

Write 410 words every day – read them and make sure they are the best 410 words you can write for that day. Don't hack at it too much at this stage. Tweak it and swap a word here and a word there. Accessorise your words and choose carefully. There is always a perfect word to match a given situation.

Wait until the whole book is finished to do the final chopping and editing. Anything you delete along the way while writing your book keep in a file. You can never get those little gems back once you have deleted them. On the other hand some gems are better off being deleted and left to their own devices in the trash. Just don't make that final decision until you have finished your book.

CHAPTER BY CHAPTER AND USING YOUR CHAPTER PLAN AS A PATTERN AND 410 WORDS PER DAY AS YOUR GOAL, BUILD YOUR STORY.

You have proven to yourself that you can do it. Now, just keep going. Take each chapter from your plan and expand on it. Tell us more. Tell us the story. Lead us through from chapter one, to chapter thirty-six. Keep writing 410 words every day. Keep asking what happens next? If you find you have written more than 410 words on any day, you still have to write 410 the next day. Extra words on a day is a bonus. You must write every day. One day you will find you've finished the novel.

Let me just tell you here that *no* publisher is going to break into your house and ransack through all your cupboards until he finds a piece of writing by you. Unlike the calls you get asking you to change telephone company or complete a tele survey, no publisher is going to pick your phone number out of the phone book and keep pestering you for a book. You have to let your writing loose into the world.

Books are a bit like children. There comes a time when you have to let them free, but only into safe hands! Choose carefully. You wouldn't lock your children in a drawer and never let them see the light of day. Don't do it with your characters. What good is a manuscript doing in the bottom of a drawer gathering dust? Brave the elements. Develop a thick skin and keep sending it off. You never know where fate is going to be lurking. And remember if it's meant for you, it'll not go by you. Get the Writers & Artists Yearbook. It's in the library. Look up agents and publishers. Look up what each one is looking for and send them exactly what they are looking for. If they only want a synopsis and three chapters just send that.

You may get many rejections you may get none. You may get a letter pointing out a tiny weakness in your novel that you can correct. You may get a wonderful letter saying that they want to read the rest of your book. You may get a follow up letter to say they want to publish it. I can tell you being published and seeing your book in print is a wonderful feeling. I wish it for all of you. Thank you for doing this workshop & workbook I hope you enjoyed it. I hope it helped you. I hope I wasn't a hard task master. This is where I bow out gracefully and leave you to treasure and nurture your words.

I know you can do it. You have all you need. Remember, we are all storytellers, you are already a storyteller. Now tell your story.

Good luck with your writing. Please invite me to your book launch.

I wish you happy days writing, always and leave you with a few thoughts from Mark Twain and T. S. Eliot and other sayings to read every day. I have also added a selection of short stories and articles written by moi which I hope you enjoy.

Lots of love, Jacinta

"Twenty years from now you will be more disappointed by the things that you didn't do than by the ones you did do. So throw off the bowlines. Sail away from the safe harbor. Catch the trade winds in your sails. Explore. Dream. Discover."

Mark Twain

"Footfalls echo in the memory
Down the passage which we did not take
Towards the door we never opened
Into the rose-garden."

T. S. Eliot

Jacinta's Magic Formula
410 (WORDS) X 365 (DAYS) = 1 (BOOK)

Repeat everyday

I AM A STORYTELLER.
I CAN WRITE 410 WORDS A DAY.
I CAN CREATE CHARACTERS.
I CAN CREATE SETTINGS
I CAN CREATE PLOT

I can create a beginning – a situation – the hook

I can create a middle – a problem – the what happens next?

I can create an end – the problem solved – the ahh factor

I can create and write a story, a novel.

I AM CREATIVE

SKIN DEEP

(published by Poolbeg 2006)

So I keep thinking. Thinking that maybe if it
hadn't been in the fool's month. And on the last day.
It was like a last chance to catch me out. One more
day and I might have been nobody's fool. So I keep
thinking. Thinking that maybe if I'd found it some
other time. Or, better still, not at all.

But I did find it. I found it by accident. Lurking.
Hiding. On the back of my knee. The right knee.
Either knee would have been the wrong one. So
it makes no difference which knee. But I keep
thinking that it does. That maybe if it had been
some other person's knee. But it wasn't. It was very
definitely my knee and the right one. And there it
was. Just waiting for me to find it. So I did a twirl.
And found it.

My husband kissed it when I showed it to him.
Kissed the little pin top imposter. Said he loved it.
Said he loved me. My friends said it was so cute,
they wished they had a beauty spot. Just like my
one. They could have mine. I didn't want it. From
the moment I saw it I didn't trust it.

"We'll have to remove it," the specialist said,
barely lifting her dark, tightly permed head. "We'll
have it off in no time." she said, licking her lips.

And she was true to her word. It took no time at
all to remove it and it was fine. No pain. No pain is
fine with me. Only three stitches.

"We'll have to wait ten days for the results but it
looks fine to me," she said as she patted me better.

So we were all fine. And that was that. It was
fine she'd said and she was the expert. She knew
what she was talking about. She knew her moles.
Knew how to excavate. Could wax poetic on all
manner of burrowing things. Especially mine. She'd
be in touch in ten days to confirm just how right she
was and how fine I was.

I nearly missed her telephone call. I answered it
just before I went out. I was all set for a bit of retail
therapy. I'd seen a dress. Very expensive. An arm
and a leg job. Glamorous. Lush. Black velvet. To my

knees. I was going to treat myself. I deserved a little treat after all I'd been through. But just before getting my treat I made the silly mistake of answering the phone when it rang. Big mistake. So silly of me.

I recognised her voice immediately. Soft, business like. I should have recognised the doom and gloom in it. But in those days I didn't know doom or gloom. I had never met them before.

"Is it about the results?" I asked stupidly.

Well, she wasn't ringing me for the good of her health, was she? Of course it was all for the good of mine. The fine results. I should have known by her tone of voice that fine wouldn't come into it. *"Don't you dare use that tone with me!"* I should have shouted at her but instead I just listened.

"I'm afraid the result of the test is A typical."

Well, well, what about that, I thought. It sounded good to me. An A. My first. I'd always wanted an A in English or History. Now I had an A in moles. An A is always good, isn't it? Well, no! On the subject of moles, an A is a very bad grade. In fact, it's a fail. And what do you get for a fail in moles? Cancer, that's what you get. But I knew I couldn't have cancer because that's what other people get. But not me.

So now she wanted to see me. Well I wanted to see her too. I could explain her mistake to her. Face to face. Tell her how wrong she was. Then we could chat about something else. The weather. The price of a pound of mince. All she wanted to chat about was how terrific she was at chopping up cancer. But I had places to go, dresses to see. Why didn't I just tell her I was busy. Too busy. *"Very busy at the moment. Very, very busy. Fully booked up for chats."* I should have said.

"In fact I can't see anyone for a cancer chat for at least twenty years. Yes. I'm sure I could fit you in then. I'll pencil you in for 2.30pm twenty years from today and you can chat about my tiny little mole then. Of course, if I have a cancellation before that I'll give you a ring. But don't hold your breath. The chances of that happening are about as remote as a young healthy mother getting skin cancer. Ha. Ha.

I'm so awfully, awfully sorry," I should have said to her. *"But you'll just have to go peddling your long, sad face and smart blue suit and matching eyes to some other poor sucker. Have a little chat with them. Pick on an older sucker. This sucker is not available. Do you hear me? Not available for you or any little bit of cancer gossip you might like to share."*

But instead I just whimpered and listened. I even agreed to see her that very day for more of a cancer chat.

I rang my husband first. He was out to lunch. Couldn't be found. Stuffing his face with some tender, juicy, cancer free flesh. With onions and all the trimmings. I rang my sister next. A sucker who's always available for a chat.

"Hi!" I whispered. "I'm all alone and I have cancer."

She was calm. Said she'd be right over. Then she told me that she loved me. Twice. I held on to the phone. Kept the connection until she arrived. Her eyes were bloodshot. Make-up streaked on her face. Black lines ran from her eyes. Like a sad clown. What had happened to her? Who had upset her? She squeezed me. Told me everything would be all right. I believed her.

In the doctor's surgery she sat beside me. Close. We closed ranks. The doctor, as promised, chatted on and on and on about moles. My big sister took tear stained notes and prayed on a string of tear drop pearls that hung around her neck. She wrote down the three types of skin cancer. Jotted down that I had the worst type. I wondered was the worst type very bad or just bad. I soon found out. The worst, is very, very bad. Another fail. Only 80% survival rate.

"And what about the other 20%?" I heard my sister ask.

Yes what about the poor unfortunate 20%?

"They don't survive." The mole doctor looked sad.

"Do they die?" I asked.

Now she looked very sad.

She nodded her head up and down and up and down. Like a bloody ornament in the back window of a car but sadder. So I decided to keep quiet. Not to make her any sadder. This was too much for her. I kept quiet. Ask no questions, be told no lies. Sit. Listen. Let my sister ask all the questions. She's always been nosey.

The sun edged it's way in the roof-light of the doctor's rooms. Listening. Waiting to hear the damage it had done. Beaming.

And I wished the wracking noise would stop. Someone's heart was being broken in this room. I could hear it. I never knew that a heart could be broken. So I was thinking, what's love got to do with it? Just words. Of songs. Figures of speech. Until now. And the sobbing. The sobbing is going through my brain. It is so very, very close. My sister crying too. Not taking notes now. Holding me and I'm sobbing. Listening. Paying attention in case of another test at the end of it all. We couldn't afford to fail another test.

We learned all manner of science and fiction. There was a satellite cell in my leg, near the original wound that had to be removed. That was all right then. Remove the satellite. They'd sent a man to the moon in one of those. He came back fine.

And where are all these tears coming from? Who knew I had so many. I wish they'd stop. They can't be coming from me. I feel nothing. Gone way beyond feeling. Orbiting the room now. Ground control to mole.

The doctor was dying to cut into me again. Cut in about a centimetre. Avoid the tendons. Then maybe do a skin graft. She was getting very enthusiastic. But what did I care. If it would cure me she could cut the whole leg off. I don't need it anymore. It's probably worn out. Past it's best before date. I've been using it now for the past thirty six years. Only thirty six.

I didn't believe her when she told me the skin would grow again. Pull the other leg, I nearly said but just giggled instead. I wondered what else would grow. More moles. A crop of them. Crop, flock, gaggle, herd, army. Please don't tell me any more. I nearly shouted in a whisper. Just do what you have to. Put me asleep. Wake me up. Better. Fixed. A cancer free zone. Please. Please.

So another something new I learned was that cancer is a frequent flyer. It travels. Goes all over the place to all sorts of exotic places. Kidneys, lungs, anywhere. It's not selective. It hops and hides. Has an open ended pass. Final destination, most desired address – the blood stream.

Some cancers are home birds. They never travel. But mine, of course mine is a traveller. I have made travelling easy. There are no borders in my body. Freedom of speech and freedom of passage are my beliefs. I will die for my beliefs. I nearly laughed but thought it would be rude so I cried some more instead.

"Melanoma. Melanoma." The doctor keeps saying it. Over and over she says it. It sounds so nice. Not like the killer it is. Cancer sounds like a killer. Shut up cancer. Let Melanoma speak. Melanoma. Soft and kind. Like semolina. Semolina, melanoma. Melanoma for the adult, semolina for the child.

And what about my child? She hasn't even had a birthday. *"Hey you, God! Do you hear me? Up there in your ivory tower with the pearly gates. Where are you in my hour of need? I flocked to mass every Sunday and hay day and holiday. Novenas, rosaries, stations of the cross. It's pay back time. I don't want this cross, God. Are you listening? Listen.*

Oh, God, what about my little baby? My little girl? Don't take me away from her. Not yet. No one loves her like I do. Loves the bones of her. Kick her, I limp. I am limping now, God. All the time. Is that not enough of a cross for you? Well come on then God, give me pain, lots of pain. I can take it."

The sobbing sound is getting worse. I can't bear it. I can't hear myself talking to God for all the sobbing I'm doing. And I can hear a pigeon too. On the roof-light. It's making that noise. You know the sound. I can hear it in-between the sobbing. And the doctor talking. Pontificating and cooing. Vying to be heard. If my cancer made a noise we could find it. Speak up cancer. Tell them where you are. Then it's open season on cancer cells. We'll bag the lot. But it's mute. Like me. Shh! Keep quiet. I might be dreaming.

There'll be a wound the doctor said. A big, kick ass, wound. She told me we'd have to mind the poor wound. Look after the poor, little wound. The wound had to be given a chance to heal. Well fuck the wound I say. What about me? Heal me. Me. And there's a free theatre tomorrow, she said. All delighted and excited, she could start cutting into me tomorrow in the free theatre, she said. Roll up, roll up, no tickets needed, standing room only. But I know I won't be in any humour to be entertained tomorrow. If there is a tomorrow.

At last my husband is here. Holding me. Didn't he get the short straw all the same. My life partner. Life. Not a chance. I can feel his guilt. He loved it. Kissed it. Befriended it. Now he's crying Judas tears. He's never cried any sort of tears before. This cancer thing is really taking control.

We've had a charmed life, him and me. No need for tears. Until now. He's all bent. Twisted. Out of shape. And for a moment, just the briefest of moments I get a glimpse of what he will be when he is old. I want to hold him. But I will never grow old. Old like them, my mother, father.

"If only." they say. "If only." They keep saying.

So I think of pots and pans and tinkers. While they talk of Padre Pio and St. Jude and maybe a little holiday. Maybe Lourdes. They calmly play let's pretend and jolly hockey sticks. And there, there everything will be all right. I wish they'd stop. But it's how they cope. I don't want them to cope.

"Look at me." I want to shout. "Show me how you really feel. Let me feel it. Scream for me. Scream. I can't. If I do I'll know it's real."

Another cry. My baby. Smiling up at me. She is the same to me. Always. Loves me for me. Warts and all. Now moles. She doesn't know what is growing in me. She has no fear. It's all in the here and now for her. And that's all I have. She puts her arms up to me. Chuckles. Wants to be held. Tight. I cling on.

Everyone is with me but I will be alone. Except for the cancer. That will be with me. Growing. Lurking. And I keep thinking that it will be loyal. It will befriend me and stay until the end. And is this the end? If it is, it is a very strange ending. Not at all how I had imagined it would be. So I keep thinking about that. You know, the end.

WAY TO GO, DAD.

Broadcast on RTÉ Radio 1 as part of the Francis McManus Awards

I married a rat. Twenty five years ago. Dressed up like a big
meringue in the Holy Rosary Church. He stayed for a decade then left.
Left me, this stinking kip and all who lived in her.

"Please, please. Don't leave us. Please think about what you're doing
to me and the children. I couldn't bear it if you left me. Don't go." I
begged. Implored the bastard not to go. Begged the bastard
to stay.

"Don't go, please. Stay. Stay. I'll do anything, anything you want."
I soothed and cajoled. Pouted and tried to look appealing and sexy in
my see- through' tears. I tried to humour him. Tempt him. Tried
everything. Begged.

"Think about all you'll be leaving behind."

"Like what?"

"Like your four beautiful children and me. Me. "

I used my most sultry tones. Sucked in my sagging stomach.
Clenched my fallen arse. Tried to remind him of steamy nights of
endless passion. Lust, sometimes love, sometimes both. Sleepless,
orgasmic nights. Not thinking of other nights. Lonely, cold. With one or
all of the beautiful children vomiting or bed-wetting. Holding them in
the darkness. Cuddling them to me. "Hush, hush, Mama's here, always
here." Keening favourite tunes and nursery rhymes. And they ranting
and raving at demons that only existed in their heads, or maybe not.

"You're right." He said as he climbed up the stairs to our bedroom
"I should think about this." He kept nodding his head. A moving
target. I wanted to take a swing at him. Draw out and hit him.
Hard. Feel my hot hand sting against his smug little face. Watch bright
pink weals rise up in the soft of the cheek that I had stroked with
tender hand before. Inflict pain for all the tortured times I had turned
to tell him that I loved him. Ignored. Forgotten. Do him damage for
all the bitter hurt I knew, deep down in my waters, he was going to
cause. To me. My children. Especially them. Bile burnt like acid. I
wretched and gagged and waited. Sitting pretty on the bottom step of
the stairs.

Five minutes later he came down. Carrying a small bag.
Neatly packed with shirts I had ironed and sexy boxer shorts I
had bought. "Well," the bastard said. "I've thought about it and
I'm definitely going."

"Why? Why are you going? What about me and the children? How
will we manage without you? Please, please don't go. I love you more
than anything." I pulled at him. He shrugged and turned away.

"I'm going. I don't love you. Nothing you can say will make me stay."

So he did. He left. Without so much as a peck on the cheek. Just one big kick on the arse for me and he was gone. Gone with all my hopes and dreams packed up tight in his small Samsonite. The big strong man carried all my weak little dreams away with him.

And week in, week out I missed him. Ached all over for him. I needed him. My body needed him. I am a man's woman. I like men, even bastards. Sex is natural for me. In out, in out. An' slow slow, quick quick, slow. Men recognise the beat. Sense the rhythm. The thrashing in me to rouse the game. The wanting. And now, when I thought the chase was done I was facing a new hunt. Raw wounds oozed. Love, hate, panic. Circling over. Watching it all. Calling out in the void of my soul. For love. Crying out for him. But he was gone. The bastard was gone. Hate is more physical than love. Sex cures love. There is no cure for hate. Only death.

Pity he didn't die. He had a bad heart. Healthy but bad. I could have coped better with death. It is the cure all. The panacea. Death is socially acceptable. Do gooders get high on it. Craw thumpers offer you craic and sympathy. Now they purr happily behind their yellowing net curtains. Congratulating, themselves on their timing. I step out, they step in again. Curious but afraid. Fearing obesity. It might be catching. A woman on the loose is a dangerous thing. Liable to pick up any ugly husband that's hanging around. No man is safe least of all yours. The bastard's safe. He's gone, good riddance to him. Or bad riddance. Why should he have anything good in his life? Let him suffer like me. Paying Peter, robbing Paul while he sits back snug. Smug in his Mammy's arms. Lullaby's of 'there there' and eat up a fine bite. My children lost two grandparents, three aunts, four uncles, one great great grandmother, endless cousins and their father all in the one day. Pruning and culling, pillaging and raping their little lives. They cried when I told them he was gone. They thought he would come back. Sometime. He didn't.

Time is cruel. Selective. Only heals some wounds. Others it leaves open. Festering. Annual reminders of anniversaries and birthdays. Time ticks off all the couple days, family days. Days it would be better to forget. But can't.

Then, after a time, one Christmas day. Peace on earth, good will to men. He rang. Not to wish me comfort and joy. Nor to deck the halls. Not bearing gifts of gold, regret or remorse. No question of many happy returns.

"Hi how's it going? How've you been?" The bastard was happy. None of my wishes had been granted.

"What do you want?"

"Any chance of a divorce?"

Two chances.

"I'll have to think about it."

"Well we could come to some arrangement about money and things. Get it all sorted out once and for all."

So after all these years. He wanted to sort it out. Sorting it out seemed reasonable when he said it. How come the bastard always sounded reasonable? Even in his finest moments of madness he seemed reasonable. It was reasonable that I had reared our four beautiful children. On my own. Always the odd one out. One of a pair is always odd. Awkward to place at a dinner table or invite to parties. So against all odds I fed and clothed us, body and soul. Shoes, coats, pyjamas, teddy bears I collected for them all. Bowed and Scraped. Encore, encore. No round of applause for living hand to mouth. Money couldn't buy what we lived on. Which was just as well. After him we had no money. Delivered from all evil. After him everything was rooted in my children. And I was rich.

On the day the bastard left. One of his children, the six year old, only six, sat on the bottom step of the stairs. Sat watching out the window. Little chestnut hands pulling at the skirt of her short blue cotton dress. Yanking it down over her knees. To her no-toes. Waiting for her Daddy. Her hair all tied up. Little gold bunches streaked with the sun. Waiting. Big blue pools when he never came. "And why not Mammy?" I gave a reasonable answer. Her brother held her. Couldn't cry or speak. He was the mute man about town now. And that was reasonable for an eight-year-old. The newborn babies slept through it all. Oblivious. Babies do that. Sleep in the afternoons. It is the reasonable thing to do. It was reasonable that I had bled and cried sewing strange dresses. For even stranger women. All sequence and glitter. For silver. Now half my home was his. It was very reasonable that he put his hat on and walked off into the sunset. To sow his seed. Go forth and multiply.

There is only one reason for wanting a divorce. Bastard mark two was on the way. The new voluptuous foetus grower wanted everything legal. The silly bitch had fallen for the same line I had. Hook, line and sinker. And sink her he would. Deep. Shards of lunacy and pain would pierce and cut her bloody heart. Crack and shatter the illusion of his perfect image.

There are no windows in the divorce courts. Just glass panels way up high for the birds. Everyone is for the birds. All in camera and not a smile to be seen. Pink, green sickly safe colours. They have tried but it is still a frightening place. I was frightened. Face to face with the unknown.

I didn't recognise the bastard at first. He knew my most intimate secrets and I didn't know him. I never knew him. I knew the smell. A persons smell never changes. I smelt the rat. Turned and there he was.

Beady little eyes staring at me. I had loved him. Once. Once he was my friend. The best.

A friend or loved one cannot be with you in the divorce courts. Only enemies and the unloved. Loneliness and sadness hang like cobwebs waiting to be swept away. Under the carpet and forgotten. No one is interested in the pedantic little details of your miserable life. The endless times you wished someone else would put on the kettle or heat the bottles. Pour a glass of wine. Break the tarnished silence. Speak so you'd hear your own voice. Watch your martyr for the cause routine.

No one likes a martyr. No matter what the cause. Details of enforced retreat and solitude are boring. So let's hail the conquering hero. The master of his own destiny. And mine. Give him half a house, let him keep all his money, forget about what he did to his children, pretend his wife doesn't exist. Decree it all. Let's hear it for the bastard. Three cheers for the big bastard.

In the divorce courts no one has a past. No one wants to remember. No blame is apportioned. Past, present, future are all together. It's all in the now and the hear ye, hear ye of the judge. Roll up, Roll up. Grab your partners for the last dance. Last chance. No jury. Just one good man and true. My face is haggard and lined standing before him. I smell of carbolic and years of clean cheap living. I am aware of every part of me. It's all scarred and hurt.

I see nicotine stains on the bastards fingers. Grape tainted teeth. The dark suit is not new. Frayed edges on the shirt. The cuff gaping open. Nothing to hold it together. And deep down, dark, in the hollow of his eyes there is a flicker. Not remorse or love. A coldness I saw one day, before, a long time ago. I shiver. The worm is about to turn again. Bolt. Leave the new love. For a new love.

The judge decrees it. All I have is mine. So I smile.

I go back to the four of them. She is sitting on the bottom stair. Blonde, hair piled high up on her head. Pulling at her mini skirt. Trying to yank it down over her knees. Fidgeting with her high platform heels. Waiting. Her brother, gentle giant, is behind her. Silent. He turns to the twins. They are tired. It has been a long day.

LOVE ME TENDER

I loved writing this story. It's a bit different to my books and some of my other short stories. It's more lyrical I think. In this story I used my two children as two of the characters. It's the only time I ever wrote about anyone I know. I just wanted my children, Alan and Lucy to have something I wrote about them. The story is completely fictional. This story is going to be published in a book of short stories published by Dodder.

James lifted the egg from the boiling water and dropped it into a blue and white striped eggcup. He spread butter thickly on two slices of toast and divided them into soldiers. With a practiced flick he beheaded the egg. Bright, sticky, yellow oozed down the side of the shell and splashed onto his cream shirt. James didn't notice. Had he noticed he would have taken up his knife and, with the skill of a surgeon, removed all traces. Just as he was about to dip a soldier, the doorbell rang.

James rarely had callers. He wiped his rough, chapped hands on a tea towel and shoved them into the pockets of his knit cardigan as he shuffled along the hallway in his slippers. He was still wearing his cap. He rarely took it off. Small wisps of white hair escaped around the edges, like cobwebs. His face had a lived in look. Weathered and leathery. He opened the door slightly to see who was there.

It was a young boy. He was animated. Big chubby cheeks and bright blue eyes.

"Hallo mister, my name is Alan an' me an' my little sister, Lucy an' mam have just moved in next door an' we have a pet rabbit called Elvis an' he just escaped an' my mam said not t' bother you but I think Elvis might be hiding in your back field can I please have a look for him?"

He finally drew breath.

He was dressed in blue shorts and bare-chested. Chest and back the colour of acorns. It was a hot, balmy, mid-summer day. But even in the heat, the boy was wearing black wellington boots. James guessed they only came off when the lad went to bed. He was amused and intrigued by the young boy.

"Of course you can look for your rabbit. Come on in, lad."

James gestured to the boy to go through the hall and into the kitchen.

"Alan? Is that what you said your name was?"

"Yes. My rabbit is called Elvis and he's gone missing. I have to find him. He's not used to the countryside."

"Right Alan. Don't you worry. We'll find him. What kind of rabbit is Elvis?"

"A white one, white with black trims. About this big." Alan held his two chubby little hands out about three feet apart.

James held in the laughter and thought it would be easy to spot this giant rabbit.

Alan looked around the kitchen taking everything in. Eyes darting around the room hopping from the row of Toby jugs on the dresser, to the fox skin rug in front of the range and the heavy cast iron boot scraper propped up against the back door, holding it open. He was hoping to see Elvis.

James tried to go quickly as he stepped out of his slippers and into his muddy gardening shoes that were resting on a sheet of newspaper by the back door.

"Have you no wellies, then?" Alan asked. "I thought all farmers wore Wellingtons?"

"Aye, they do. You're right there lad, but I left mine off in the shed and we're in too much of a hurry to catch your rabbit for me to go and get them. These shoes will have to do."

James could hardly keep a straight face. His half-acre garden was hardly a farm.

They searched through the flowerbeds and shrubs but there was no sign of the rabbit. The boy kept calling:

"Elvis, come on Elvis. It's me... Alan. Come on."

Elvis was turning a deaf ear, staying where he was.

"I know he's here somewhere, mister." The little boy's lip started to quiver and his eyes moistened. James knew that any minute now there'd be tears. He put his hand on the young boy's head and ruffled the blonde silky hair.

"Tell you what!" he said "Let's you and I stay very, very quite. If that rabbit thinks it's safe he'll come out and I bet he'll head straight for my new vegetable plot over there."

James pointed to a row of bright green, inviting lettuce shoots. They waited, watching. Sure enough, in no time at all, a little pink wriggling nose appeared from behind the apple tree. James pointed and held his fingers to his lips. The boy stayed quiet. The rabbit felt secure and hopped out, stopped, wriggled his nose then hopped again. Straight for the lettuce. James stared at the rabbit. He couldn't take his eyes off Elvis. He had never seen a rabbit like it. It was huge. A huge white rabbit with a long tuft of pitch black fur right on the top of his head. The black fur was so long that it fell over to one side. His four paws were also covered in masses of black fur. He was definitely wearing his blue suede shoes. No doubt about it, the rabbit was aptly named. The little boy ran up to it and picked it up by the scruff of the neck. If the rabbit had opened his mouth there and then and launched into a rendition of "Love me Tender" James wouldn't have been in the least bit surprised.

"You were right mister, he must like your lettuce. That's prob'ly why he came in here. We don't have lettuce in our garden. In fact, we have nothing only weeds. My Mam says it's a pure God forsaken wilderness, whatever that is! Anyway the wilderness is on her list. She has this list you see, list of jobs we have to tackle. It's a mighty long list an' the garden is a long, long way down. We have to do all the mending and fixing in the house first. Whitewashing and painting. My Mam says that the windows are ready to fall out and all for the want of a lick of paint. Imagine that mister. Imagine, all the windows falling out. She says we'll never be done fixing. But my mam's great at fixing things."

"Oh, I'm sure you're a great help. With your wellingtons and everything. I'd say you give your Daddy a grand help to do all the jobs around the place. Sure you'll have them done in no time".

"Oh no. My Dad doesn't do the jobs. My Mam does all that. My dad doesn't live with us anymore. He lives with some lady. He comes to visit us on Saturdays. Well, on the Saturdays that he can. When he's not too busy. My Dad's very, very busy you know. He works in an office. I'm going to be a farmer when I grow up."

James was taken aback by the honesty and innocence of the child. He could also see the deep hurt the young boy felt but was too young to understand.

"Alan, Alan" James could hear the lad's mother calling.

"Come on, Alan, your Mam is looking for you." James said "You'd better get off home. I'm glad we found Elvis. Would you like to take a few fresh eggs in for your Mother?"

"Yeah. She's always using eggs to make cakes for me and my sister, Lucy. She makes great cakes."

After they collected the eggs, James waved Alan goodbye. For the rest of the evening he smiled to himself every time he thought of young Alan and Elvis. He hoped the young boy would call again soon. If truth be told James missed people. Missed the sound of laughter and shouting around the place. He had never married but he regarded his nieces and nephews as his own children. They used to call to visit him all the time when they were younger. Now they were grown up and spread to the four corners of the world. They wrote often and sent photographs and postcards from exotic places. They'd never believe him when he told them Elvis had moved in next door!

Early next morning James went out to collect the eggs.

"Hi mister." He heard the friendly voice and was delighted to see Alan's little face peeping in between the hedge.

"Hi Alan, how's Elvis?"

"He's ok. My mam said that the next time he escapes he's finished –

rabbit stew, she said. So, I have him on a lead. I'm keeping close tabs on him."

"If you have your wellingtons on you and Elvis could come over and give me a hand to collect these eggs."

"Of course I have my wellies on."

Alan squeezed his small body between the gap in the hedge. It was more of a struggle to squeeze Elvis through.

"We could put a gate in here." Alan called, finally pulling the rabbit through and landing on his bottom with the effort of it all.

"You know, a gate for when me and Elvis come over to see you. It would be much better than me having to shove him in through the hedge all the time."

"Well that's a great idea, Alan, let's put it on the list."

They collected the eggs, put down fresh straw, checked the vegetable patch and picked a huge bunch of sweet smelling flox for Alan's mother.

"My mam will love these." Alan said, staggering behind the huge bouquet. His mam came out to meet them at the gate.

"Alan, they're brilliant." She leant forward and gave her son a kiss as she took the flowers. She ruffled Elvis's fur.

"Hi. I'm Hope. You must be James from next door. I've heard all about you. Thanks for these, the smell reminds me of happy times." She smiled as readily as her son.

She was a tiny person. Small, gentle featured. Her skin was tanned. Hands red and wrinkled from washing. She wiped them on her jeans and shook James's hand. Then offered him tea and freshly baked Madeira cake. The air was thick with it. James couldn't refuse. Especially when he saw the little girl, Lucy. She was sitting on a big, bright patterned, rug on the kitchen floor. Looking as though any second now she would take off, carpet and all, on some exciting adventure. Her baby blue eyes flashed mischief. She was wearing a pretty blue summer dress but it was covered in sticky crumbs. Everywhere was covered, even her bare toes. She smiled a two-toothed grin up at James, her little face lit up with the delight of a stranger in the camp. She grinned at him again and rubbed the chunk of cake she was eating all over her head. Into her tight blond curls, making a halo around her head. She chuckled and James chuckled with her.

"Oh, Lucy, what will I do with you." Hope said. But she was smiling as she wiped Lucy's fat little hands and face. Alan giggled. James loved it all. Lucy chuckled again. Planning her next trick, James thought.

"You have the place lovely. It's very colourful." James pointed to the jugs of wild flowers and the vibrant fire engine red, yellow and cobalt blue cushions scattered on the armchairs and couch.

"Oh, it's just cosmetic. I have a lot to do on the place but I'm getting there." Once again the easy smile caught James by surprise.

"Listen, I love pottering around fixing things and I have lots of spare bits of timber and stuff in my shed and too much spare time so I was thinking......"

He was sipping his tea, being careful not to appear to be interfering.

"I'd be happy to give you a hand to repair some of the windows and things. It'll give me something to do and if Alan was my helper I'd really enjoy it"

"Please, Mammy, please. Can I be James's helper?"

Lucy clapped her hands and chuckled. She was all on to be a helper too.

"Well, if you're sure you don't mind..... and you'd have to let me know the minute you got fed up with us... and.."

"I promise I'll let you know." James winked at Alan, then at Lucy.

And so, the pattern began. Alan called into James every morning and helped him to collect the eggs. Then they carried the wood, tools and whatever else they needed back to Alan's house. The hammering, gluing and fixing began. Alan handing up the nails, marking the wood and generally watching every move James made, hanging on his every word.

"Sh, Sh," James, would say.

"Do you hear that bird, Alan? That's a bullfinch. Listen."

"Look I see him. He's over there."

On the really hot days they went up beyond the back field to get ice-cold water in the well. Exploring everything, listening for crickets, spotting butterflies on the way. The well was half hidden under a huge flat stone, surrounded by ferns. James held Alan tightly and let him stretch out flat on his belly against the damp cold earth to scoop out the icy water. A special friendship and trust grew between the two of them. An unlikely pair. The young and the old, both in their wellingtons. By now Alan had acquired an old cap belonging to James. It was too big for him but he loved it. It kept the sun out of his eyes and he felt more like a farmer.

Sometimes, in the evenings Alan would call into James and watch him tie flies for fishing. Hair, feathers, wax, varnish and pliers all spread out on a newspaper on the kitchen table. James's failing eyesight not a hindrance – he could tie flies with his eyes shut. Alan's favourite was a pheasant-tail nymph tied from the feather of a cock pheasant.

On very special balmy warm evenings. Alan's mother let him stay up late. James packed a flask and sandwiches into the fishing bag and took a big torch from the top of the dresser and they headed off to a sheltered spot on the edge of the river. Their "lucky" spot. Alan unraveled the line as James attached the fly. James wielded the rod like a whip and the fly came alive, hopping on the water, making little circles along the river. Almost immediately he was rewarded with a hefty trout. Young Alan could hardly contain himself; he helped with the landing and weighing. Ignoring the midges as they landed on his appetising, juicy skin. He never flinched, absorbed in the magic of the river by torchlight. James's leathered skin was immune to the insects. They fished, neither talking, both comfortable in each other's company. Always.

The repair work continued. During the day and Alan's mother made bright curtains and more cushions. In no time at all the house was transformed.

Lucy surprised them all by taking her first few steps.

"Time for her to get wellie boots." James said as they all clapped. He was delighted he'd been there when Lucy walked. Lucy was chuffed with herself and the reaction of her audience. She went for encore after encore.

With the house finished James and Alan turned their hands to the garden. The God forsaken wilderness. They tackled it in small sections. The first thing on their list was a hutch for Elvis. They built a big run all around it. Alan made a sign "Gracelands" to hang on the outside.

Then they dug a little vegetable patch and planted lettuce, Elvis's favourite. James transplanted clumps of flox and lupins from his own garden into two big flowerbeds on either side of the cottage door.

And all the while the two friends grew closer. The boy stopped talking about his father's busy life and started to enjoy his own. James was never too busy. There were no more lonely times for either of them.

The days grew shorter and the young boy swapped his tee shirt for a jumper. They still headed off on their walks, talking all the time. Heads nodding in unison.

"Well lad," James said to Alan one day when winter had definitely moved in and the smell of turf knitted into their clothes.

"You've done well. You've done a great job with the cottage. All the mending and fixing are finished now. I bet your mam's right proud of you now the fixing's all done. "

"Oh, she is, mister, I heard her tell my nana on the phone. She told my nana all about it and all about you and all about my fishing and guess what! My nana's coming down to stay for a while."

"Oh, she'll get a right surprise when she sees all the fixing you've done, Alan."

"Yeah, I'm glad she's coming, she's the one who bought Elvis for me. She even gave him his name, it's after her favourite singer. She's always singing, especially Elvis songs. She even grabs me and does funny dances. She's real funny."

"I can't wait to meet her. She sounds like just what this place needs."

"You know you're wrong about all the fixing being done, mister. It's not all done yet. My mam has another bit of fixing planned. I heard my Mam talking to my Nana. I heard her tell my Nana that she was going to fix her up with the lovely fella next door. That's you, you know."

And then Alan gently slipped his soft little hand into James's and the only sound to be heard, as the two pals trundled off down the lane, was the clump, clumping of their wellington boots and a very loud guffaw from James.

THAT'S LIFE

First published by Woman's Way

My nerves are gone. I am a basket case. Weeping and gnashing of teeth are my new hobby. I am starting to enjoy and even take pleasure in the gnashing. I could weep and gnash for Ireland in the Olympic Games. I have considered taking valium, in a sandwich, toasted or open, bit of coleslaw on the side.

I'm not the only one suffering. Hundreds before me have suffered. Indeed hundreds after me will suffer. I take no comfort from this. I don't care who suffers as long as it isn't me. I should be rolling out the barrel and kicking up my heels. Engaging in a bit of debauchery and inappropriate behaviour. I should be standing in my Rob Roy kilt; arms held high Mel Gibson style, crying "FREEDOM" to the top of my voice. Instead I am deep down in there in the valley of tears. Life looms ahead like the Jack Lynch Tunnel only someone seems to have turned the lights off.

"And what has her so upset?" I hear you ask in your most sympathetic tones. "What can possibly be causing the poor woman such grief?" I hear you wonder, in your usual compassionate way. Well let me confide in you. It's my children, the two young adults. I suppose you thought as much. Well they have been busy packing up their bits and pieces for the past few months now. They will be leaving tomorrow. I will sorely miss them. The house will be so empty. Like all mothers, I knew this day would come. Secretly I hoped it never would. I'll miss the buzz, the chats the mess and the noise about the place.

My nearest and sometimes dearest thinks I have finally lost it. He wants to celebrate the peace and quiet, order champagne and act like sixteen-year-olds. God if he only knew what sixteen year olds get up to. Maybe we could both do with a bit of that. Anyway, he's planning romantic meals and nights away in luxury castles.

He doesn't understand how I feel. No one does. I seem to be the lone voice roaring and shouting in the wilderness. I know that major worrying is called for in this situation. Anyone who says they don't worry when their young adults leave the nest is lying. Big time.

So I will weep and gnash and wallow proudly in the valley of tears while my two young adults and all the other young adults they hang around with are off on a fortnight's holiday. Soaking up the rays, giving it loads and throwing shapes on some sun kissed, white beached Mediterranean island. They won't be back in the bosom of the family for two whole weeks. Sure it's enough to make any mother cry.

THAT'S LIFE

Published by Woman's Way

I have just realised that I have the perfect body. This, as you can, I'm sure, appreciate is an outstandingly good piece of news since I have spent the second half of my life trying to lose half of my body weight without, I am obliged to admit, much success. Now I am pleased, chuffed even, to tell you that there is, in fact, nothing whatsoever wrong with my body. My body is perfect. I just live in the wrong hemisphere. You see, I should be one of the Walbiri women of Australia. There the women spend half their lives making their boobs, bums and thighs bigger. The bigger they are the sexier they are. I would be one dangerous Walbiri woman.

Unfortunately, by accident of birth, I most definitely blame my parents for this, I am living in the part of the world that dictates I must be stick insect like, emaciated even. An appearance I surrendered six months before the birth of my oldest child. It all went downhill from there. Oh Yes, that's another thing I am not responsible for. It is my children that are directly responsible for my present size. If they hadn't been so big and bonny to begin with. If they hadn't left half eaten dinners, half chewed Mars bars and in latter years half consumed bottles of plonk lying around, forcing me to eat and drink I would be fine.

But now I must rely on camouflage, nothing like a touch of war paint to boost the confidence and improve the prospects. In fact, I go nowhere without my make-up. I applaud Elizabeth Arden, Revlon, Max Factor and Estee Lauder. I number them among my closest friends. I bring them everywhere. I blush in their presence. I am a shadow of my former self when they are around. I am eternally grateful to all of them.

I am also grateful that I was not born a Surma woman of Ethiopia. While I respect their customs, and would defend their right to have such customs, there is no way I'd have a wooden plate inserted in my lower lip. The bigger the lip the more chance you have of getting a man. Now I'm great at giving lip but having one large enough to hold all my personal belongings is just that little bit beyond what I am prepared to do to please a man, any man. Neither am I prepared to have my earlobes stretched till they're banging off my shoulders, flapping in the wind and catching in everything. I am quite prepared to forgo this even if it means that I lack sex appeal.

Anyway, and I promise I'm really not being a bit smug here, I have it on the strictest confidence that at least one particular very delightful, gorgeous even, human being of the male variety, grant it a very biased on, thinks me and all my bits are sexy the way they are. So lets hope he stays in that blissful state of ignorance for another while yet.